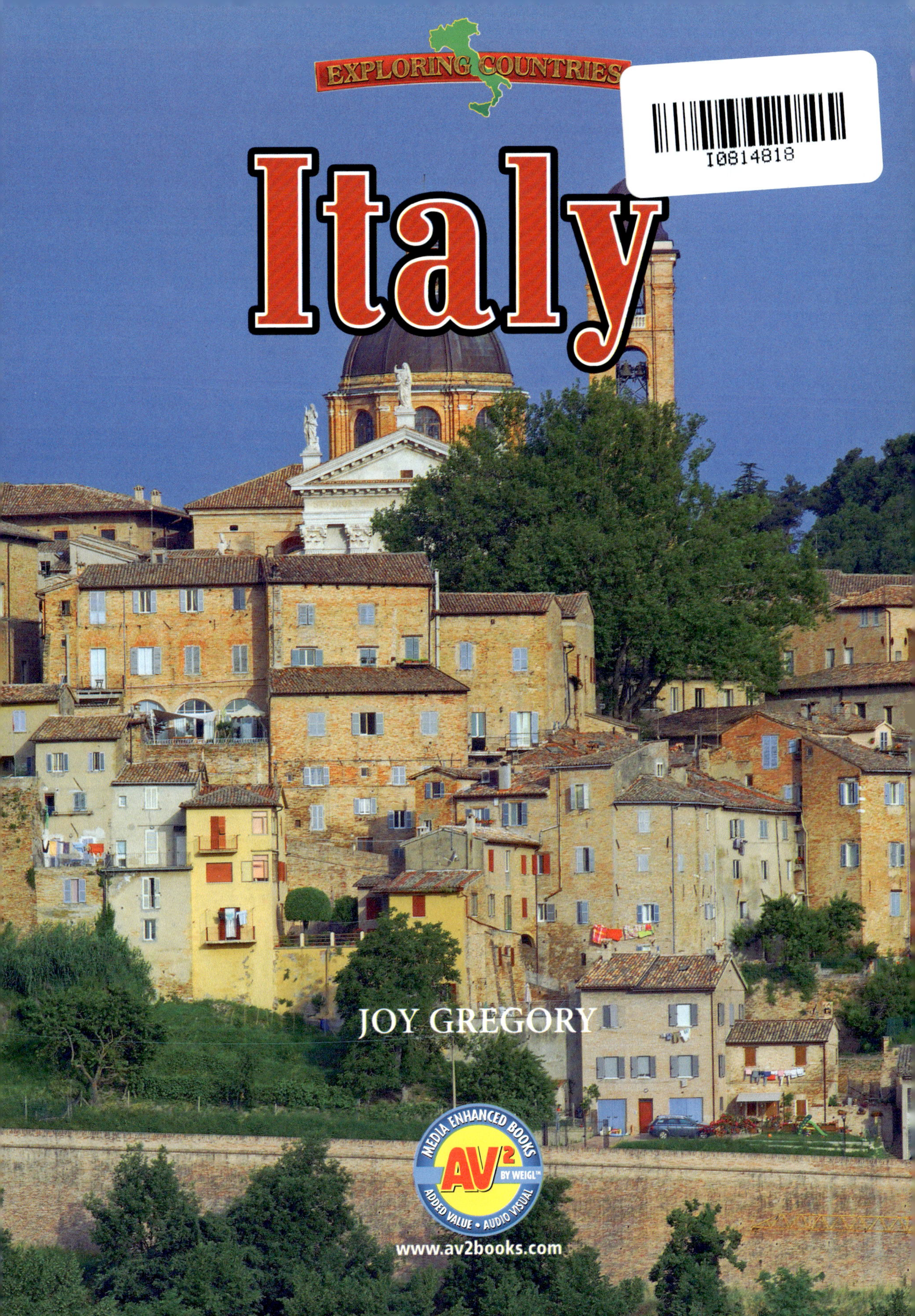
EXPLORING COUNTRIES
Italy
JOY GREGORY
MEDIA ENHANCED BOOKS
AV2 BY WEIGL
ADDED VALUE • AUDIO VISUAL
www.av2books.com

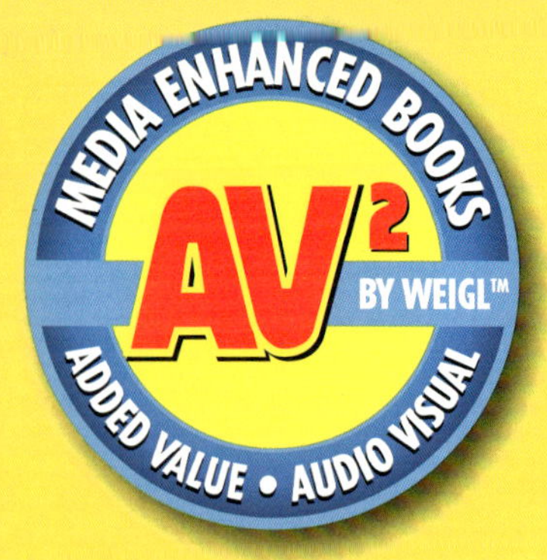

Go to www.av2books.com, and enter this book's unique code.

BOOK CODE

M939576

AV² by Weigl brings you media enhanced books that support active learning.

AV² provides enriched content that supplements and complements this book. Weigl's AV² books strive to create inspired learning and engage young minds in a total learning experience.

Your AV² Media Enhanced books come alive with...

Audio
Listen to sections of the book read aloud.

Key Words
Study vocabulary, and complete a matching word activity.

Video
Watch informative video clips.

Quizzes
Test your knowledge.

Embedded Weblinks
Gain additional information for research.

Slide Show
View images and captions, and prepare a presentation.

Try This!
Complete activities and hands-on experiments.

... and much, much more!

Published by AV² by Weigl
350 5th Avenue, 59th Floor
New York, NY 10118
Website: www.av2books.com

Library of Congress Cataloging-in-Publication Data

Names: Gregory, Joy, author.
Title: Italy / Joy Gregory.
Description: New York, NY : AV2 by Weigl, 2017. | Series: Exploring countries | Includes bibliographical references and index.
Identifiers: LCCN 2016047212 (print) | LCCN 2016047520 (ebook) | ISBN 9781489654144 (hard cover : alk. paper) | ISBN 9781489654151 (soft cover : alk. paper) | ISBN 9781489654168 (Multi-user ebk.)
Subjects: LCSH: Italy—Juvenile literature. | Italy—Description and travel--Juvenile literature.
Classification: LCC DG417 .G678 2017 (print) | LCC DG417 (ebook) | DDC 945—dc23
LC record available at https://lccn.loc.gov/2016047212

Printed in the United States of America in Brainerd, Minnesota
1 2 3 4 5 6 7 8 9 21 20 19 18 17

022017
020117

Project Coordinator Heather Kissock
Art Director Terry Paulhus

Photo Credits
Every reasonable effort has been made to trace ownership and to obtain permission to reprint copyright material. The publishers would be pleased to have any errors or omissions brought to their attention so that they may be corrected in subsequent printings.

Weigl acknowledges Getty Images as its primary photo supplier for this title.

Contents

Italy Overview

Italy, a country in southern Europe, is easy to identify on a map. Most of the country is a peninsula that is shaped like a boot and extends into the Mediterranean Sea. Italy, which has one of Europe's largest **economies**, has been important since ancient times. Officially called the Italian **Republic**, the country became a **democracy** in 1946. Italy includes diverse regions, with their own histories, cultures, and cuisines, or types of food. The national language is Italian, but much of the population speaks a regional **dialect**. The land is mountainous and rugged, with several active volcanoes. Italy is known for its ancient ruins, historic monuments, vibrant cities, charming towns, and beautiful countryside.

Portofino, in northern Italy, is one of many towns built into the hillsides or cliffs that line parts of the Italian coast.

Basilicas, or large churches, with beautiful domes are found in cities throughout Italy.

Gelato, a soft Italian ice cream, comes in many flavors.

Italians take part in various religious festivals during the year.

Groves of olive trees, which grow well in Italy's soil and climate, are a common site in the countryside.

Exploring Italy

Italy covers 116,348 square miles (301,340 square kilometers). From north to south, the country measures more than 700 miles (1,100 km) long. The Adriatic Sea borders Italy to the east. The Tyrrhenian Sea is to the west, and the Ionian Sea lies to the south. These three seas are part of the Mediterranean Sea. In northern Italy, France lies to the west, and Switzerland and Austria are to the north. Slovenia is to the northeast. Italy includes two major islands, Sicily and Sardinia, and several smaller islands. San Marino and Vatican City are within Italy but are not part of the country.

France

Rome

Spain

The Blue Grotto

Mediterranean Sea

Map Legend

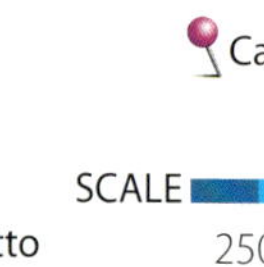

Capital City

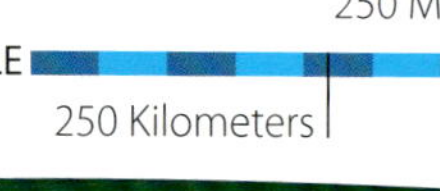

Rome

Rome is the capital and largest city of Italy. It was founded more than 2,500 years ago. Today, more than 3.7 million people live in Rome.

The Blue Grotto

The Blue Grotto is a natural limestone cave on the north shore of the island of Capri. An underwater opening allows sunlight to enter, creating an intense blue light inside the cave.

Mount Etna

Mount Etna is the highest active volcano in Europe. Located on the island of Sicily, it rises 10,968 feet (3,343 meters) above sea level.

Lake Garda

Lake Garda, in northern Italy, is the country's biggest lake. It covers 143 square miles (370 sq. km). The lake is 34 miles (54 km) long and as wide as 11 miles (18 km).

LAND AND CLIMATE

The Italian landscape is mostly hills and mountains with some **plains**. Mountains higher than 2,300 feet (700 m) occupy more than one-third of Italy. The country's two large mountain ranges are the Alps and the Apennines.

The Po River, in northern Italy, drains an area of about 27,000 square miles (70,000 sq. km).

The Alps extend east-west along Italy's borders with France, Switzerland, Austria, and Slovenia. Within the Alps are Italy's highest peaks, which are part of Monte Bianco and Monte Rosa. However, the highest point of Monte Bianco is located in France, where the mountain is called Mont Blanc. Monte Rosa's highest point is in Switzerland. Monte Bianco di Courmayeur, the highest peak entirely in Italy, is 15,633 feet (4,756 m) high.

The eastern portion of the Italian Alps is called the Dolomites.

The Po River, which starts in the Alps, is Italy's longest river. The Po River is more than 400 miles (645 km) long. It flows east from the French Alps and empties into the Adriatic Sea on Italy's east coast.

The Apennines run down the center of the Italian peninsula. They are about 870 miles (1,400 km) long and from 25 to 125 miles (40 to 200 km) wide. These mountains were formed by the movement of **tectonic plates**. These shifts also are responsible for the country's many earthquakes and for its volcanoes. Italy has three active volcanoes, Mount Vesuvius, Mount Etna, and Mount Stromboli.

The Italian coastline varies from rocky cliffs to white sandy beaches. The five villages of Cinque Terre, which means "Five Lands" in Italian, are built on the cliffs of a coastal region in northwestern Italy called the Italian Riviera. Several of Italy's most popular beaches are found on the island of Sicily.

Italy's climate differs from north to south. The northern part of the country experiences cold winters, with snow. In southern Italy, winters are milder. Summers are hot and humid throughout the country but warmest in the south.

Land and Climate BY THE NUMBERS

86 Degrees Fahrenheit

Average daily high temperature in Rome during July and August. (30° Celsius)

9,554 Feet Height of Monte Corno, the highest peak in the Apennines. (2,912 m)

4,712 Miles

Length of the coastline of Italy. (7,600 km)

PLANTS AND ANIMALS

Italy is home to a variety of plant and animal **species**. Cypress, European olive, and cork oak trees grow in the lower regions of the Alps. Tree species such as larch and Norway spruce thrive at higher elevations. However, only certain plants, such as mosses and lichens, are able to grow above the **snow line**. Trees in the Apennines include oak, beech, chestnut, and pine.

Flowering plant species found in Italy include an evergreen shrub called oleander. Other examples are myrtles, holly, and lily. The lily is Italy's national flower.

Some animal species have become rare or **extinct** as population and settlements have grown. Types of animals still found in the Apennines include the Apennine wolf and the lynx. The chamois is a small goatlike animal hunted for its meat and hide. The Marsican bear is an **endangered** species of brown bear. Today, this species lives only in Abruzzo National Park in the mountains east of Rome. A **venomous** snake called the asp viper is also found in the Apennines.

Plants and Animals BY THE NUMBERS

Fewer Than 50
Number of Marsican bears living in Italy.

MORE THAN 150 YEARS
Life span of cork oak trees.

30 MILES PER HOUR
Top speed reached by a chamois. (50 km per hour)

Hundreds of chamois live in Abruzzo National Park.

NATURAL RESOURCES

Rich soil is one of Italy's most valuable natural resources. It helps Italian farmers grow a variety of crops. Most of Italy's farms are located in the south or in the Po River Valley. These include vineyards, or farms that grow grapes used to make wine. Italy is a world leader in both wine and olive oil production. It also grows wheat, corn, tomatoes, sugar beets, rice, soybeans, citrus fruits, cherries, apricots, and nectarines.

Fish are plentiful in the seas around Italy. Sardines, tuna, and anchovies are the most valuable saltwater fish. Trout and eel, found in the country's rivers and lakes, are Italy's most common freshwater fish. About 10 percent of the fish consumed in Italy are caught inland.

Italy has a number of valuable minerals. They include rock salt, lead, manganese, zinc, mercury, potash, sulfur, and bauxite. Italy is a leading producer of pozzolana and feldspar, minerals used to make cement and concrete. Building stone, particularly marble, is mined in Italy. The country also has some natural gas and crude oil **reserves**.

Natural Resources BY THE NUMBERS

23% Portion of the land in Italy that is used for growing crops and raising livestock.

2nd Italy's rank among the world's wine-producing countries, after France.

1920s Decade when natural gas was found in the Po Valley.

600 MILLION Number of barrels of crude oil reserves in Italy. (95 billion liters)

Brilliant white marble is mined in Cararra, Italy.

TOURISM

More than 48 million foreigners visit Italy every year, spending about $40 billion in the country. They tour ancient ruins, art museums, and religious sites featuring the work of Italian artists such as Leonardo da Vinci. Italy has many **UNESCO** World Heritage Sites. Examples include historic city centers, as well as buildings such as the Leaning Tower of Pisa.

The Santa Maria del Fiore cathedral in Florence is also called the Duomo after its huge dome.

Two of Italy's most visited sites are the Colosseum and St. Peter's Basilica. The Colosseum, built in about AD 70, is an **amphitheater** in Rome. Hand-to-hand combat between fighters called gladiators entertained thousands in this stadium. St. Peter's, completed in 1667, is part of Vatican City. The Roman Catholic Church's headquarters, Vatican City is within Rome. It is home to some of the world's finest art, including the Sistine Chapel **frescoes** by Michelangelo.

In Florence, tourists visit the Santa Maria del Fiore cathedral, built in the **Gothic** style. Other popular tourist destinations are the city of Venice and the ruins of Pompeii. The Grand **Canal** and other canals are the main streets of Venice, built on islands on the Adriatic coast. In Pompeii, near the city of Naples, tourists see an ancient town preserved in volcanic ash after an eruption of Mount Vesuvius in AD 79.

Poor construction caused the Leaning Tower of Pisa, a white marble bell tower completed in the 14th century, to start tilting even before it was finished. Today, more than 1 million people each year visit the unusual structure.

Italy has many ski resorts. Most are located in or near the Alps. The most popular resorts are Cortina d'Ampezzo, site of the 1956 Winter Olympic Games, and Corvara, where World Cup ski races are held.

Warmer temperatures bring hikers to the same mountains. In central Italy, tourists rent mountain bikes to tour the Tuscany region's rolling hills, olive groves, and vineyards. At Fucecchio Marshes, near Florence, birdwatchers can see 200 species, including white, gray, and purple herons.

Seaside resorts, originally fishing villages, line the western, eastern, and southern shores of the Italian peninsula and nearby islands. Vacationers relax on the beach, canoe, sail, windsurf, and scuba dive. Traveling to some resorts, such as Portofino, requires a boat ride.

Italy's excellent food and high fashion attract people from around the world. They enjoy delicious seafood and local cheeses, homemade pasta dishes, espresso coffee, and *zeppola*, a fried pastry. Shops in Milan sell clothes and leather goods by the best Italian designers.

Tourism BY THE NUMBERS

291 Number of ski resorts in Italy.

51 Number of World Heritage Sites in Italy.

2 Miles Length of the Grand Canal in Venice. (3 km)

The 15th-century town of Pienza, in Tuscany, is a UNESCO World Heritage Site.

INDUSTRY

Italy has the fourth-largest economy in Europe, after Germany, France, and the United Kingdom. Manufacturing is a large industry in Italy. It employs 28 percent of the country's workers. Most of Italy's manufacturing companies are located in the north near the cities of Milan, Turin, and Genoa.

The country's top **exports** are machines, engines, and motor vehicles. Fiat is the largest car manufacturer in Italy. Maserati, Ferrari, and Lamborghini are luxury automobile brands produced in the country. Other companies make and export agricultural and earthmoving machinery and equipment for metal-working and food processing businesses.

Italy's textile industry is one of the world's largest producers of fabric and yarns. Textile companies work closely with the Italian fashion industry. Italy is known for its luxury clothing brands, and these companies also produce footwear, handbags, and luggage. Well-known brands include Versace, Prada, Armani, Fendi, and Dolce & Gabbana.

Industry BY THE NUMBERS

25.5 MILLION Number of workers in Italy.

1899 Year the Fiat company was founded.

2 Number of times each year Milan Fashion Week is held, when designers show their new clothing styles for women.

The Huracán, released by Lamborghini in 2016, can travel a maximum speed of 201 miles (323 km) per hour.

GOODS AND SERVICES

Italy's service industries contribute about three-quarters of the total value of goods and services produced in the country. Workers in these industries provide services instead of making goods. Teachers, nurses, government employees, shopkeepers, and restaurant chefs are service workers. Italy's largest service industry is tourism. More than 3 million Italians have jobs related to providing services for tourists.

Italy was one of the original six members of what is now called the **European Union** (EU). The EU was formed to make it easier for its members to trade, or **import** goods from and export goods to one another. The EU also establishes rules to improve conditions for workers in member countries.

EU members Germany and France are Italy's leading trading partners for both imports and exports. The United States, the United Kingdom, Spain, and Switzerland are other major buyers of Italian exports. China does not buy many Italian products, but it is the third-biggest seller of foreign goods to Italy.

Goods and Services BY THE NUMBERS

1958 Year Italy joined what became the European Union.

68% Portion of Italy's workers in the country's service industries.

10TH Italy's world rank in annual exports by country.

$409 Billion Annual value of Italy's imports.

In Italy, chefs prepare food in *pizzerias*, local restaurants called *trattorias*, and fine dining *ristorantes*.

ANCIENT PEOPLES

Tens of thousands of years ago, people lived in the hills and caves of the Italian peninsula. Little is known about those early peoples. By 700 BC, the Etruscans lived in the region now called Tuscany. Roman tribes, including the Latins, lived in the central and southern portions of the peninsula. Greek traders had established settlements in many coastal areas.

The Etruscans were farmers and fishers. They tried to seize the Greek settlements in their area. They also fought against the Roman tribes.

After the Romans defeated the Etruscans, the kingdom of Rome was established. In 509 BC, the Roman Republic replaced the kingdom. During the republic, citizens were involved in how they were governed.

The Roman Republic lasted more than 450 years. During this time, the **city-state** of Rome became powerful. By the time the republic ended, Rome controlled most of Italy, as well as Syria, Macedonia, Greece, and Egypt and Carthage in North Africa. Under the republic's last leader, Julius Caesar, Rome took over the ancient region of Gaul. Gaul included France, Belgium, and parts of Germany.

Ancient Peoples BY THE NUMBERS

736 BC
Year Greek traders established the city of Syracuse on the island of Sicily.

12 Number of city-states set up by the Etruscans.

April 21, 753 BC
Date that a legend says Rome was founded by brothers Romulus and Remus.

The second temple of Hera is one of the world's best-preserved ancient Greek temples. It was built in Paestum, on the Tyrrhenian coast, in about 460 BC.

THE ROMAN EMPIRE

The Roman **Empire**, with Rome as its center, was established in 27 BC. Augustus Caesar was its first leader, or emperor. The Roman Empire lasted longer than any other in the world. It also became the world's largest empire. Its territory included most of western and southern Europe, most of Great Britain, parts of northern Africa, much of the Middle East, and land as far east as Armenia.

Many Roman emperors were cruel and unfair, and several were murdered. However, emperors also oversaw the growth of the empire, from city planning to the development of laws. Road and sewer systems were designed to serve the community's needs. Theaters and public libraries were built.

The Roman Empire was defeated by German invaders in AD 476. The defeat is called the Fall of Rome. The eastern part of the empire, known as the Byzantine Empire, survived for many years. Political control of the western region was split among warring groups.

The Roman Empire BY THE NUMBERS

More Than 1 Million
Number of people living in Rome by about AD 100.

50,000 MILES Length of the road system built during the Roman Empire. (80,000 km)

About 50,000
Number of seats in the Roman Colosseum.

In the 2nd century AD, the Romans constructed an outdoor theater in Pompeii. The Teatro Grande was large enough for an audience of about 5,000.

CONFLICT AND UNIFICATION

By the time the Roman Empire ended, it had already lost control of some distant regions. After the Fall of Rome, parts of present-day Italy were divided into city-states. The Huns, Franks, and Lombards, groups from other areas of the empire, led most of these city-states for a time.

The Frank king Louis the Pious ruled much of today's western Europe, including parts of northern Italy, from 814 to 840.

The Roman Catholic Church was a powerful force in the western part of the former empire. Some city-states were loyal to the pope, the head of the Church. Others fought for independence from **papal** rule.

By the 12th century, the independent city-state of Venice had become rich and powerful, based on its trade with Asia and other areas. Wealthy local families in central and northern Italy also gained power. The Medicis, known as the House of Medici, ruled Florence and later all of Tuscany from about 1430 to 1737. The House of Sforza ruled Milan from 1450 to 1535.

In Milan, the House of Sforza developed industry, supported artists, and built large churches and castles. Sforza Castle is one example.

The pope continued to rule a large area of central Italy, known as the Papal States. For centuries, foreign powers such as France, Spain, and Austria ruled most of the south. Austria controlled some areas in northern Italy as well.

In the 1800s, there were efforts to unite Italy and free it from foreign and papal rule. In 1859, a soldier and patriot in northern Italy named Giuseppe Garibaldi led an army in a war against Austria. The following year, Garibaldi organized a rebellion in Sicily and Naples that united most of Italy. Victor Emmanuel II became the first modern king of Italy in 1861.

For decades, the Kingdom of Italy was led by a king but governed by elected representatives. In 1922, Benito Mussolini took control of the country. Mussolini ruled as a dictator, making all government decisions and permitting few individual freedoms. During World War II, which lasted from 1939 to 1945, Italy sided with Germany and Japan against the **Allied Powers** before its defeat in 1943. Italian citizens who supported the Allies forced Mussolini from office. In 1946, Italians voted to end the **monarchy** and established a republic with democratic elections.

Conflict and Unification BY THE NUMBERS

5th Century AD
Time when people fleeing from German invaders established settlements that became the city of Venice.

1469–1492
Years Lorenzo de' Medici, known as Lorenzo the Magnificent, ruled Florence and supported many artists and writers.

About 1,000
Number of soldiers who fought with Giuseppe Garibaldi in 1860.

At the battle of Calatafimi in Sicily on May 15, 1860, Giuseppe Garibaldi and his soldiers defeated the army of the king of Naples.

POPULATION

Italy has a population of more than 62 million people. The country is densely populated. This means it has, on average, more residents per square mile (sq. km) than many other countries. Italy has 546 people per square mile (211 per sq. km), compared to only 92 people per square mile (35 per sq. km) in the United States.

Most Italians live in or near **urban** areas. After Rome, the biggest city is Milan, with more than 3 million people. Naples has about 2.2 million residents. About 1.8 million people live in Turin. Almost half of the country's population lives in the Po River Valley.

Italy has an aging population and a low **birth rate**. About 14 percent of the population is younger than 15 years old, and 21 percent is older than 65. The number of births in Italy is lower than the number of deaths. These trends mean the country's population is likely to decline in future years.

Population BY THE NUMBERS

69% Portion of the Italian people who live in cities and towns.

About 675,000
Population of Palermo, the largest city in Sicily.

214 Number of countries and territories with higher birth rates than Italy.

About 7 million people live in the metropolitan area known as Grande Milano, or "greater Milan."

POLITICS AND GOVERNMENT

Italy's constitution has been in effect since 1948. Under this constitution, the government has three separate branches. They are the executive, legislative, and judicial branches.

The executive branch includes a prime minister, a **cabinet** called the Council of Ministers, and a president. The prime minister, who is appointed by the president, leads the Council of Ministers. The president is elected by a group of government officials and serves a seven-year term.

The legislature, or parliament, is made up of two houses, the Senate and the Chamber of Deputies. There are 315 senators and 630 deputies. Often, the prime minister is a leader of the political party with the most seats in the Chamber of Deputies. Italian laws must pass both houses of parliament. Members of the legislature are elected by the people to five-year terms. To hold office, deputies must be at least 25 and senators must be at least 40 years old. In the judicial branch of government, the supreme court is Italy's highest court.

Politics and Government BY THE NUMBERS

1946
Year that women in Italy voted for the first time.

50 Years Old
Minimum age to serve as president of Italy.

2014
Year that Matteo Renzi, at 39, became the youngest prime minister of Italy. He served for two years.

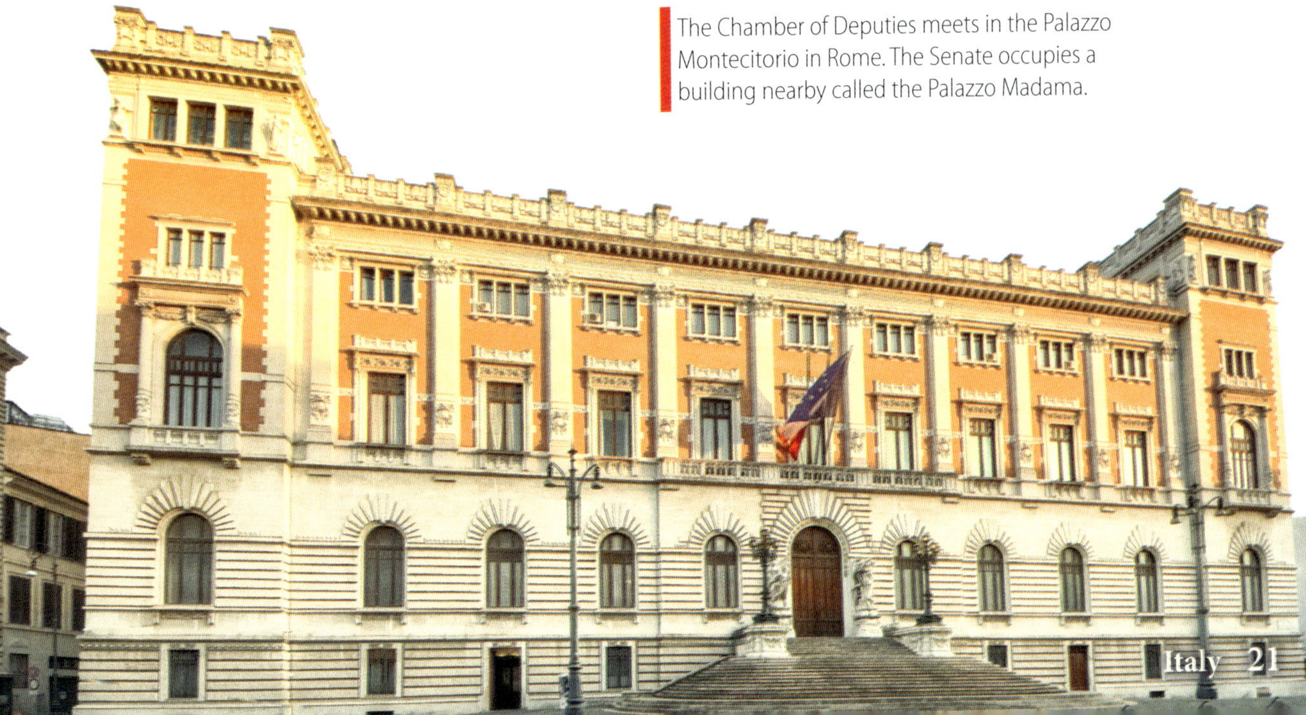

The Chamber of Deputies meets in the Palazzo Montecitorio in Rome. The Senate occupies a building nearby called the Palazzo Madama.

CULTURAL GROUPS

Most people in Italy are of Italian descent. Often, their families have lived in the country for many centuries. The Italian population also includes people whose **ancestors** came from other parts of Europe, including Germany, France, Slovenia, Albania, and Greece.

About 500,000 migrants, including many women and children, have arrived in Italy since 2014.

In the 21st century, large numbers of people affected by wars in the Middle East and Africa have fled to Italy. Most of these **migrants** traveled to Italy by boat from North Africa. Some have stayed, and others have continued on to other parts of Europe.

For most people in Italy, Italian is their native language. In communities that border other European countries, many residents speak the language of the neighboring country, such as German, French, or Slovene. People on the islands of Sicily and Sardinia speak different variations of Italian. Other parts of Italy with distinct dialects include the region of Calabria, at the southern end of the Italian peninsula, and the areas around Naples, Venice, and Milan.

The people of Sardinia have their own dialect, culture, and music. Sardinian music is often played on a woodwind instrument called the launeddas.

Most Italians are Roman Catholic. Smaller numbers of Italians practice other Christian religions, Judaism, or Islam. There are more than 1 million Muslims in Italy. About one-fifth of people in Italy believe in or are committed to no religion.

There are various religious holidays in Italy. Many of them honor Catholic saints, or holy people. Italians celebrate saints at the Madonna della Bruna Festival in the city of Matera and during San Biago Day in the town of Aventrana. People eat homemade bread baked in the shape of a cross on St. Joseph's feast day and sweet buns called *cuccia* on St. Lucy's feast day.

On Good Friday, an Easter parade called the Procession of the Mysteries takes place in western Sicily. Groups of people carry wooden religious statues through the town of Trapani for almost 24 hours. It is one of the oldest religious events in Italy.

Cultural Groups BY THE NUMBERS

1984 Year that Roman Catholicism ceased to be Italy's official religion.

More Than 800
Number of mosques and Muslim prayer rooms in Italy.

MORE THAN 28,000
Number of Jews living in Italy.

More than three-quarters of the Italian population is Christian, although not all attend church regularly.

ARTS AND ENTERTAINMENT

The leaders of ancient Rome and early Italian city-states supported the creation of beautiful public buildings, monuments, and artworks. Some of the greatest artists in history lived and worked in Italy during the Renaissance. This period of scientific, artistic, and cultural development in Europe began in the early 14th century and continued until the late 16th century. Italian Renaissance painters and sculptors include Leonardo da Vinci, Michelangelo, Sandro Botticelli, and Raffaello Sanzio da Urbino, known as Raphael. Much of their work is on display in museums, art galleries, and churches across Italy.

Leonardo da Vinci, who lived from 1452 to 1519, was one of the leading scientists of his time as well as a successful artist.

Italy is also the birthplace of opera, a drama set to music. Italian composers of opera and other classical music include Antonio Vivaldi, Niccolo Paganini, Giuseppe Verdi, and Giacomo Puccini. Luca Francesconi, born in 1956, and Oscar Bianchi, born in 1975, compose classical music today.

On display at the Uffizi Gallery in Florence are many of Sandro Botticelli's works, including the painting *Allegory of Spring*.

Leading Italian opera singers, such as Andrea Bocelli and Cecilia Bartoli, record and perform throughout the world. Opera houses in the Italian cities of Viareggio, Verona, and Taormina hold annual opera festivals. Other music festivals feature classical music in Siena and jazz in Umbria every year. Each summer, the Tuscan city of Lucca hosts a rock-and-roll music festival.

Italian-made films hold the record for winning the most Academy Awards in the best foreign film category. Italy hosts one of the world's oldest film festivals. The Venice International Film Festival takes place every summer.

Today's artists and writers also advance Italian arts and entertainment. Every major city in the country has contemporary art galleries. Artists Mario Schifano and Pietro Cascella show their innovative work in Gibellena, Sicily. Italian poet Giosué Carducci won the country's first Nobel Prize for Literature in 1906. In 2016, the novels of the Italian writer with the **pen name** Elena Ferrante sold more than 1 million copies in the United States.

Arts and Entertainment BY THE NUMBERS

1778 Year Milan opened its opera house, Teatro alla Scala.

1932 Year the Venice International Film Festival was founded.

11 Number of Academy Awards won by Italian films for best foreign picture.

6 Number of Italian writers who have won the Nobel Prize for Literature.

Opera singer Cecilia Bartoli has sold more than 10 million audio and video releases of her work.

SPORTS

Soccer, known in Italy as football, is the country's most popular sport. Millions of Italians play for fun and follow the country's national and professional teams. A game similar to soccer called *calcio fiorentino*, or "Florentine kick," was invented in Italy during the 16th century.

Young men in Renaissance-style costumes play *calcio* for their neighborhoods as part of the Feast of St. John, as they have since the 1500s.

Italy's men's national soccer team won its first World Cup in 1934. Since then, the men's team has won the 1938, 1982, and 2006 World Cups. Italy's national team wears blue and white uniforms decorated with the Italian flag.

Italy has hosted the Olympic Games three times. After the 1956 Winter Olympics in Cortina d'Ampezzo, Rome hosted the 1960 Summer Games. In 2006, Turin welcomed international athletes to the Winter Olympics.

A number of Italian athletes have been Olympic champions. Diver Klaus Dibiasi won three gold medals in the 1960s and 1970s. Fencer Edoardo Mangiarotti earned 13 Olympic medals for Italy. Italian athletes won one gold and six silver medals in fencing at the 2016 Summer Olympics in Rio de Janeiro, Brazil.

Gianluigi Buffon, born in 1978, is considered one of the greatest goalkeepers of all time.

Alpine ski racer Alberto Tomba is nicknamed La Bomba for his speed. Tomba won three gold medals at the 1988 Winter Olympics in Calgary, Canada. Cross-country skier Stefania Belmondo competed in five Olympics from 1992 to 2002. She won two gold, three silver, and five bronze medals. Italy's success in skiing continued with Christof Innerhofer's two medals at the Winter Olympic Games in Sochi, Russia, in 2014.

Automobile racing, basketball, and competitive cycling are popular in Italy. Italian-made cars compete in national and international auto-racing events. Champion Italian race-car drivers have included Alberto Ascari, Alberto Colombo, and Andrea Bertolini. The country's national basketball league is one of the best in the world. Italy has produced several world-class cyclists. Two Italian cyclists won medals, including a gold medal for Elia Viviani, at the 2016 Olympics in Rio.

Sports BY THE NUMBERS

2ND Italy's rank as the country with the most soccer men's World Cups, after Brazil.

20 Number of teams in Italy's best professional soccer league.

201 Number of Italian athletes at the Rio Olympics in 2016.

14 Number of times Team Ferrari has won the Formula One auto racing championship since 1950.

In 2016, Elia Viviani won an Olympic gold medal in the omnium, which consists of six cycling events.

Mapping Italy

We use many tools to interpret maps and to understand the locations of features such as cities, states, lakes, and rivers. The map below has many tools to help interpret information on the map of Italy.

Mapping Tools

- The compass rose shows north, south, east, and west. The points in-between represent northeast, northwest, southeast, and southwest.
- The map scale shows that the distances on a map represent much longer distances in real life. If you measure the distance between objects on a map, you can use the map scale to calculate the actual distance in miles or kilometers between those two points.
- The lines of latitude and longitude are long lines that appear on maps. The lines of latitude run east to west and measure how far north or south of the equator a place is located. The lines of longitude run north to south and measure how far east or west of the Prime Meridian a place is located. A location on a map can be found by using the two numbers where latitude and longitude meet. This number is called a coordinate and is written using degrees and direction. For example, the city of Rome would be found at 42°N and 13°E on a map.

Map It!

Using the map and the appropriate tools, complete the activities below.

Locating with latitude and longitude

1. Which city is found at 44°N and 11°E?
2. What mountain is located at 41°N and 14°E?
3. Which large city is found on the map using the coordinates at 45°N and 9°E?

Distances between points

4. Using the map scale and a ruler, calculate the approximate distance between the cities of Rome and Naples.
5. Using the map scale and a ruler, calculate the approximate distance between Milan and Venice.
6. Using the map scale and a ruler, calculate the approximate distance between Turin and Bari.

ANSWERS 1. Florence 2. Mount Vesuvius 3. Milan 4. 120 miles (190 km) 5. 150 miles (250 km) 6. 540 miles (870 km)

Quiz Time

Test your knowledge of Italy by answering these questions.

1 What is the highest peak entirely in Italy?

2 How long is the Po River?

3 What is the national flower of Italy?

4 When was the Colosseum built?

5 Who was the first emperor of the Roman Empire?

6 When did Benito Mussolini take control of Italy?

7 What is the population of Italy?

8 What is Italy's highest court?

9 How many Muslims live in Italy?

10 When was *calcio fiorentino*, or "Florentine kick," invented?

ANSWERS

1. Monte Bianco di Courmayeur
2. 400 miles (645 km)
3. Lily
4. About AD 70
5. Augustus Caesar
6. 1922
7. More than 62 million
8. Supreme Court
9. More than 1 million
10. 16th century

Key Words

Allied Powers: the group of countries, including the United States, Great Britain, the Soviet Union, and France, that fought against Germany, Italy, and Japan during World War II
amphitheater: a theater with different levels of seats in a circle around the stage
ancestors: people in one's family in past times
birth rate: the number of children born per thousand people in a country's population
cabinet: a group of government officials who advise a prime minister or president and who often head different government departments
canal: a waterway built for navigation, draining wet areas, or watering land
city-state: an independent state that includes a city and the surrounding land
democracy: a type of government in which people choose their leaders by voting
dialect: a form of a language spoken in a certain area or by a specific group of people
economies: the wealth and resources of countries or areas
empire: a nation or territory headed by a single ruler
endangered: at risk of becoming extinct
European Union: a political and economic organization of more than two dozen countries
exports: products that are sold to other countries
extinct: no longer surviving in the world or in a certain area
frescoes: wall or ceiling paintings done on fresh moist plaster
Gothic: a style of architecture common in Europe from the 1100s to the 1500s
import: to bring in goods from another country or area
migrants: people who move from one country or region to another
monarchy: a government headed by a king or queen
papal: relating to the office of the pope
pen name: a false name used by a writer
plains: flat, treeless areas
republic: a form of government in which the head of state is elected
reserves: the amount of a mineral available for future use
snow line: the elevation above which some snow remains throughout the year
species: groups of individuals with common characteristics
tectonic plates: sections of Earth's surface that move very slowly
UNESCO: the United Nations Educational, Scientific, and Cultural Organization, whose main goals are to promote world peace and eliminate poverty through education, science, and culture
urban: relating to a city or town
venomous: describing an animal that uses a poisonous substance

Index

Log on to www.av2books.com

AV² by Weigl brings you media enhanced books that support active learning. Go to www.av2books.com, and enter the special code found on page 2 of this book. You will gain access to enriched and enhanced content that supplements and complements this book. Content includes video, audio, weblinks, quizzes, a slide show, and activities.

AV² Online Navigation

Audio
Listen to sections of the book read aloud.

Book Pages
AV² pages directly correspond to pages in the book.

Video
Watch informative video clips.

Embedded Weblinks
Gain additional information for research.

Key Words
Study vocabulary, and complete a matching word activity.

Try This!
Complete activities and hands-on experiments.

Quizzes
Test your knowledge.

Slide Show
View images and captions, and prepare a presentation.

AV² was built to bridge the gap between print and digital. We encourage you to tell us what you like and what you want to see in the future.

Sign up to be an AV² Ambassador at www.av2books.com/ambassador.

Due to the dynamic nature of the Internet, some of the URLs and activities provided as part of AV² by Weigl may have changed or ceased to exist. AV² by Weigl accepts no responsibility for any such changes. All media enhanced books are regularly monitored to update addresses and sites in a timely manner. Contact AV² by Weigl at 1-866-649-3445 or av2books@weigl.com with any questions, comments, or feedback.